Masterpiece

[signature]

PSM. 38:15

Masterpiece

Seeing yourself as
God's work of art
changes everything!

Dr. Ken Nichols

Copyright © 2014 by Dr. Ken Nichols

All rights reserved.
Scripture quotations in this publication are from *The Holy Bible, New International Version*, Copyright © 1978 by International Bible Society. Used by permission of Zondervan Bible Publishers.

Also quoted:
Holy Bible. New Living Translation, copyright© 1996, 2004, 2007 by Tyndale House Foundation. Used by permission of Tyndale House Publishers Inc., Carol Stream, Illinois 60188. All rights reserved.

ALIVE Counseling Ministries
P.O. Box 176
Forest, VA 24551

ISBN: 978-1-888237-96-2
Cover design and interior formatting by Anne McLaughlin, Blue Lake Design, Dickinson, Texas
Published in the United States by Baxter Press

For we are God's masterpiece. He has created us anew in Christ Jesus, so we can do the good things he planned for us long ago.
—The apostle Paul, in the letter to the Ephesians,
New Living Translation

This book is dedicated to our three precious children: Mark Alan, Kendra Kay, and Kara Lynn. One of the great joys of parenting is to watch the maturing process in your children. Each of our children has followed a unique path designed by God to reflect His image in who they are and what they do. Whatever human limitations they may have are opportunities for the Master Artist to make brush marks of eternal value as they are His masterpiece in the making.

Mark is a committed family man, active in his local church, a loyal and caring friend and is committed to excellence in his life and law enforcement career.

Kendra loves to encourage her family and friends with unique insights from the Word, has the gift of encouragement and has an authentic spiritual joy that is contagious.

Kara is a genuinely sensitive person who cares especially for those struggling with life issues, she is a creatively gifted writer/ editor and her blog, www.poeticpetitions.com is appreciated by many.

We love you very much!
Dad and Mom

Contents

Acknowledgements 9

Chapter 1   Who Am I? 11

Chapter 2   A Flawed Portrait 23

Chapter 3   The Artist's Touch 43

Chapter 4   A New Image Takes Shape 61

Chapter 5   The Finished Portrait 81

Endnotes   94

Alive Resources 96

Acknowledgements

This project was truly a team effort. Thank God for those who faithfully provided financial support, editorial input, and valuable suggestions.

I am especially grateful for Pat Springle, President of Baxter Press, for his competent editing and insightful writing. Pat added biblical and practical content that captured the essence of how God's grace radically reshapes our self-image. His writing skill and editing handiwork are threaded throughout this book. Carol Lacy provided professional direction for the first edition and her ideas, spiritual wisdom and practical suggestions remain in this copy. Marlene, my faithful wife and ministry partner, always offers encouragement, practical suggestions and spiritual discernment. My children also provided valuable feedback and important insights that were included in the final copy.

CHAPTER 1

Who Am I?

Jesus came to announce to us that an identity based on success, popularity and power is a false identity—an illusion! Loudly and clearly he says: "You are not what the world makes you; but you are children of God."
—**Henri Nouwen**

Every aspect of our lives—every interaction, every hope, every fear, every choice, and every habit—is shaped by our answer to the piercing question, "Who am I?" We try so hard to be somebody, to be noticed, to stand out . . . or we may try to avoid standing out in any way. When we succeed and win awards and applause, our hearts swell with pride. When we fail, we feel ashamed, insecure . . . "less than." Many of us experience whiplash between these two emotional extremes, sometimes in the same hour!

Nagging thoughts of self-doubt come in many different forms. As I've asked people probing questions in my counseling office, coffee shops, and everywhere else I've talked with them, I've heard people say things like this:

"I try so hard, but I don't seem to ever measure up. I feel like a loser."

"When I look in the mirror, I feel disgusted. I'm sure others feel the same way when they see me."

"Failures from long ago still haunt my mind."

"Today's failures are bad enough!"

"I feel like I'm always on a treadmill . . . running to please people but never getting anywhere."

"I feel euphoric and powerful when I help people but I feel terrible when I fail . . . or when I try but they don't appreciate my efforts."

"If people really knew me, they'd laugh or walk away."

"If I could just _____ (fill in the blank), then I'd be really happy. But it never seems to happen for me."

"I carry deep hurts that I can't talk about."

"If you knew the truth about me, you'd walk away and never want to see me again."

We may respond to our sense of inadequacy in very different ways. Some of us think we can gain the approval we long for by doing whatever it takes to please people; others are driven to succeed in business, sports, or some other venture to prove they have value; and still others try not to make any waves at all—they think being invisible is the best way to find safety.

You must be thinking, "There has to be a better way!" There is. We can have a secure, strong, "bullet proof" self-concept based on the unfailing, unconditional love of God. We were made for relationships. We get our greatest joys, and we suffer our deepest hurts in relationships. The ultimate connection, the one that we're all made for, is an intimate, supportive, strong relationship with God. When the

There is. We can have a secure, strong, "bullet proof" self-concept based on the unfailing, unconditional love of God.

wonder of the love, forgiveness, and acceptance of Jesus Christ floods our hearts, his love begins to dissolve the conflicted messages that have clouded our minds for so long.

Perspective Changes Everything

The more we experience the depths and heights of God's affection, we'll more fully appreciate his transforming brush strokes on the canvas of our lives! In fact, *everything changes*:

- God knows even the worst about us, and he loves us still, so we no longer have to hide our secrets from him.

- New confidence in God's purpose for our lives gives us hope even when things don't go the way we hoped they'd go.

- Criticism no longer crushes us. We're more resilient, and we actually welcome input.

- When we go through hard times, we experience a "peace that passes understanding" because we're convinced we're in God's strong and loving hands.

- We realize God has uniquely crafted us with talents and abilities we can use to touch people's lives and make a difference.

- When we fail, we're not devastated. We experience regret and sorrow when we know we've failed God and hurt others. But instead of reacting to blame others or suffer prolonged shame, we respond by thanking God for his abundant forgiveness and asking, "What can I learn from this mistake or sin?"

- When we succeed, we're grateful that God gave us the ability to do well.

- We no longer obey God's rules out of guilt or fear of being punished. Instead, we obey because we want to please Jesus, the one who obeyed to the point of death for our sake.

- When people hurt us, we forgive out of the overflowing well of our experience of God's amazing forgiveness.

- We enter relationships with a full heart of love, so we have plenty to give instead of always using people to fill up the emptiness in our hearts.

Do you want to live this way? Of course you do. We all do. Maybe you think it's impossible. I have good news: It's very possible. God has given us precious and magnificent promises to count on, but it takes courage to trust him instead of the negative voices we've allowed to dominate our lives for so long.

Not long ago, I talked with Juliana, a woman who told me she had struggled for years with a deep sense of inadequacy. As we talked, I asked her to tell me more of her life's story. She gave a series of facts and dates, but I could tell she was holding something back. I asked, "Juliana, I sense you're not telling me something. And it may be something you haven't told anyone for years."

My comment surprised her. It was a gentle invitation for her to be more open and transparent about her life-shattering secret. After stammering for a few seconds, she said, "Dr. Ken, I haven't told anyone about this for over twenty years." Her voice trailed off. She was trying to find the courage to speak the words that had haunted her. I waited patiently. After a minute or two, she took a deep breath and said, "I . . . I had an abortion when I was eighteen." She burst into tears and continued, "I knew it was wrong, and I've felt terrible since then."

I'm pretty sure she assumed I would point a boney finger at her and utter guilt-generating condemnation. Instead, I said, "Juliana, thank you for trusting me with your secret. I know that was very hard to do. I'm deeply honored. You don't need to tell me about the situation, but please, help me understand how the feelings of guilt and relentless sorrow have affected you."

She looked up from her tear-soaked hands and said sadly, "The voices . . . the voices have tortured me." Suddenly she looked at me, started to laugh, and said, "No, no, Dr. Ken . . . I don't mean *that kind* of voices!" We both appreciated the momentary relief from the sobering conversation we were having. I did know that the "voices" she referred to were not flowing from some form of psychosis, but from over twenty years of not being able to forgive herself, and feeling unable to embrace the forgiveness of the Lord Jesus.

Juliana had lived with harsh, critical, condemning, hopeless voices for over half of her life. Sometimes she heard only a faint whisper and other times a distracting and deafening chant. The Adversary (Satan, the enemy of our souls) specializes in replaying devastating images of past failures and nagging, critical voices in our minds as a way of causing spiritual paralysis and emotional despair. Juliana had read the Bible for years and listened to many messages about the forgiveness of Jesus Christ, but the condemning voices in her head had drowned out the loving voice of God. That day, her courage to talk about them began a journey of healing and hope. Gradually, she regained her identity as a dearly loved, completely forgiven daughter of the King!

Juliana's story reminds us all that, no matter the nature of the failure or sin, nothing is beyond God's forgiveness and his promise to restore our image into his likeness. It's God's promise, not our past, that makes the difference.

All of Us

People at every stage of their lives wrestle with how they see themselves. Consequently, they can become obsessed with how others see them. They instinctively (and constantly) ask, "Who am I? Do I matter?"

- Adolescents ask, "What's my place in the scheme of things?" "Do I belong?" "Who can I trust?"

- Young adults ask: "Who believes in me?" "Who shares my values and purpose?" "Does anyone want me as a spouse or friend?"

- Middle adults ask: "What difference do I make?" "What's my real purpose?"

- Older adults ask: "What's my legacy?" "What lasting impact have I had on others? How can I make my life count now . . . before I'm gone."

Some of us are older, but we're still in the emotional stage of adolescence. We're still intuitively asking the questions about our identity we asked when we were in high school! When an identity rooted in the unfailing love of God fills our hearts, it takes away the need to manipulate people to meet our needs. As our self-concept becomes more secure and anchored in the promises of God, we can truly love people.

When we're insecure, we enter relationships primarily *to meet our needs and to see what we can get*; when we're secure and see ourselves as God's work of art, we lovingly invest in the lives of others with authentic transparency.

People who feel insecure don't feel confident enough to have rich, real relationships. They wear masks to hide, say and do things designed to impress, or try to intimidate others to be "one up" on them. As Christians, we don't typically wear masks to deceive others, but to protect our own inner fears and insecurities. As people become more confident and secure, they gain wisdom about who to trust (and who they can't trust), they stop playing games to win approval, and they form authentic relationships with genuine trust, respect, and affection.

One of my favorite characters in the Bible is Moses. We usually think of the mighty man of God standing in front of Pharaoh or the Red Sea and seeing God perform miracles—and those of us of a certain age invariably think of Charlton Heston in that role! But the story goes back farther than those moments of miracles. Before God met him at the burning bush, Moses considered himself to be a consummate loser. He had lost every shred of self-confidence. He was insecure and hopeless. All of his potential had been eroded by a river of self-doubt. The story of Moses, then, is the wonderful saga of God reshaping tragedy and failure into strength and joy. God overwhelmed Moses with his forgiveness and gave him a new sense of identity. He was no longer focused on his personal limitations and painful failures; he now represented the glory of Almighty God! With his new identity, God used him to accomplish some of the greatest feats in human history.

> As Christians, we don't typically wear masks to deceive others, but to protect our own inner fears and insecurities.

And if God can do that with Moses, he can do it with you and me. We'll see more of this transformation later in the book.

The Divine Artist

In Paul's letter to the Christians in Ephesus, he tells them about the immeasurable grace of God to rescue us out of sin's clutches and into the arms of God. The power of the gospel, though, doesn't stop the day we trust in Christ as our Savior. The love of God continues to melt the hard parts of our hearts and uses the brushstrokes of difficult circumstances to mold us into people who reflect the kindness, wisdom and strength of God. Paul wrote, "For we are God's masterpiece. He has created us anew in Christ Jesus, so we can do the good things he planned for us long ago" (Ephesians 2:10 NLT).

Masterpiece. That's how God sees you and me. Incredible, isn't it? It seems beyond comprehension that the God of glory, the Creator of all and our Savior would consider us to be his masterpieces—but that's how he sees us. In this book, we will uncover the Bible's truth about this wonderful concept. We'll use the metaphor of a portrait to describe how God uses the "paints" of his grace, wisdom, power, and love to give us a new, God-given identity.

Our new identity is based only and always on the unconditional, unmerited grace of God. It's not based on our performance, so we can't gain more by performing well, and we can't lose our identity as God's beloved children by failure and sin. It's not based on our appearance, so those who are handsome or pretty aren't more acceptable to God than those of us who are less attractive. It's not based on intelligence, so those with intellectual limitations aren't at a disadvantage at all.

God's grace is counterintuitive. Everything else in our lives is based on our performance, appearance, intelligence, or some other metric— everything but grace. God's amazing love and acceptance isn't just unconditional; it's *counter*-conditional. We deserve God's judgment, but God "lavishes" his grace on us and makes us his own. Does the idea of God's grace make you shake your head because it seems too good to be true? If not, you probably don't understand it yet. Throughout history, men and women who have tasted even a little of God's love have been blown away by the wonder of it! When we "taste and see that the Lord is good" and he has adopted us as his own dear children, the Spirit of God begins to change us from the inside out. Increasingly, we want to be with God and delight in him, we want to honor him in everything we say and do, and we want to follow his directions because we're sure he is far wiser than we are. In other words, our new identity changes everything. And it all starts with God's Word. God's Word influences how I see myself. How I see myself influences how I live. How I live reflects God's artwork on the canvas of my life.

Some might read these words and think, "Well, I'm doing fine. I don't need a major makeover of my self-concept. I'm on my way to the top and feeling fine!" Maybe . . . for now. God has a way of getting our attention and waking us up to our need for him. Sooner or later, failure, rejection, and heartache make us realize our desperate need for forgiveness and a new, divinely directed makeover of how we see ourselves.

Many people read these words and have the opposite response. They exclaim, "You don't know where I've been or what I've done! God has probably given up on me. I sure have." The good news is that God is the divine Artist who uses the dark colors of our lives as a background to highlight the light of his love and his good purposes for us. The blemishes of our life portrait are often the source of our greatest blessings.

No matter how badly we've blown it or how devastated we are by the wounds of others, God never wastes our pains or our sins. If we'll trust him, he'll use even those things to continue fashioning us into his glorious image . . . and ultimately, a beautiful masterpiece.

In *The Safest Place on Earth,* my friend, author and counselor Larry Crabb, described the dramatic change that happens when our identity is based on the unconditional love of God. We're never alone. Our minds may be clouded by all kinds of negative messages from the past, but the Holy Spirit patiently and tenderly communicates the heart of God to us:

> **God's Word influences how I see myself. How I see myself influences how I live. How I live reflects God's artwork on the canvas of my life.**

"I assume the Spirit is always whispering, 'Abba,' to God's children, assuring them that they are safe in His care. And he is continually calling them to become what God saved them to be, solid people, indestructibly alive, hurting perhaps, but consumed with pleasing the Father."[1]

At the end of the chapters, you'll find some questions, exercises, and a prayer. If you need more paper to write your answers, use a small notebook for your reflections.

Consider this . . .

1. How do you think most people answer the self-reflective question, "Who am I?"

2. What are some negative messages that can cause spiritual and emotional paralysis? Which of these trouble you the most?

3. Look at the list of characteristics under "Everything Changes." Which two or three of these are most attractive to you? Which seem beyond reach? Explain your answer.

4. Paraphrase Ephesians 2:10. Do you see yourself as God's masterpiece? Why or why not?

5. What do you hope to get out of this book? What difference do you hope this book will make in your life?

A prayer . . .
Lord Jesus, I want to see myself as your masterpiece. Help me be honest—with you and with myself—about my reluctance to believe you love me so much. Today, I open my heart to you and ask you to . . .

CHAPTER 2

A Flawed Portrait

The Lord works through deeply flawed people, since He made so few of the other kind.
—**Timothy B. Tyson**

It's not just "those people" who struggle with their identity. To some extent, all of us do . . . including me. I've listened to the condemning "voices within," and as a consequence, I've endured self-conscious doubts and feelings of insecurity and inadequacy. At least to some extent, one of the reasons we develop a demanding, compulsive personality style is to compensate for these negative messages. But there's hope! When we're honest about our blemishes, God can make something beautiful from them . . . yes, even our sins, flaws, and defects. It's a mark of his great grace.

A negative self-image produces a wide variety of problems—in all areas of life, from mild to severe. As a counselor, I've met with people who are ruthlessly driven to succeed to prove themselves (to their parents, their peers, or themselves), and I've comforted those who have given up on life because they've concluded there's no hope that anyone will ever love them or notice them. Those who have internalized negative messages may suffer from diagnosable problems, such as eating disorders, serious depression, paranoia, or narcissism, or they may experience more common difficulties, such as strained or broken relationships, outbursts of anger, the epidemic of cosmetic surgery, loneliness, and shame. In his book, *Search for Significance*, Robert McGee noted, "We develop elaborate defense mechanisms to block pain and gain significance. We suppress emotions; we are compulsive perfectionists; we drive ourselves to succeed, or withdraw and become passive; we attack people who hurt us; we punish ourselves when we fail; we try to say clever things to be accepted; we help people so we will be appreciated; and we say and do countless other things."[2]

The beginning point for a new self-image is to be brutally honest about the flaws in the one we have now. We are conditioned to deny our distortions, blame others, or find a myriad of excuses, and sometimes we learn to live in the safety of self-designed allusions or culturally imposed delusions. All of these keep us from hearing God's messages of love, forgiveness, and acceptance.

Sometimes, our self-image delusions are a bit embarrassing. I have an insatiable sense of humor and on occasion it gets me in trouble. But it's worth it because I've found that humor can be a lubricant for building relationships. Some time ago when I was recovering from rotator cuff surgery, I had an appointment with my physical therapist. As two ladies worked on my shoulder, one of them suddenly exclaimed, "Wow, what a hunk!"

I couldn't resist this opportunity. I sat up and assured them, "'Ladies, I mean really! I appreciate it, but after all, I'm a married man!"

They broke is hilarious laughter. Of course I was aware that they'd been looking out the window at a handsome, muscle man mowing the lawn!

Our Current Canvas

When God paints a beautiful portrait of our new identity, he doesn't start with a blank, clean canvas. There's already a lot of paint applied in our attempts to make ourselves look competent, attractive, popular, and powerful. Part of God's creative process, then, is to scrape away the old so he can apply the new. We can't just add the new identity to the old one. We have to do the hard—and often painful—work of identifying our previous attempts to form our own identity apart from God. No one is exempt from this process. Even those who have been Christians for years need to be rigorously honest about our natural inclination to form our identity on performance, appearance, and intelligence.

Powerful Messages

So it begs the question . . . where do these manipulating and incriminating messages come from? Our self-concept is the product of complex and powerful forces—forces that are so pervasive that we don't even realize their impact on us. The Bible identifies these as the world, the flesh, and the devil. These aren't completely separate enemies; they work together to take our eyes off the grace of God and distort the portrait God is painting. Let's look at these.

The world

The easiest way to understand the impact of our culture is to see the power of advertising. Hundreds (if not thousands) of times a day, we're bombarded with messages that persuade us we can't be happy and fulfilled unless we have this product or that service. A single ad may not make much of a dent, but the carpet bombing of advertising promises has deceived us to the impact of all the messages! Advertising is based on a huge secondary lie. The toothpaste may clean your teeth, but what's the real, implied promise of the ad? It's that the toothpaste will work magic so that you'll have the man or woman of your dreams. In his insightful book, *The Technological Society*, Jacques Ellul observed that advertising creates the false expectation of an ideal life of popularity, affluence, and fun. The problem is that almost everybody believes these assertions. Many people pursue the phantom ideal at the expense of godly values, real relationships, and genuine purpose in life.[3]

The goal of advertising is to create a need (actually a demand) for products and services. Ultimately, ads create a false but attractive image of an ideal life that's always just out of reach. In an article posted on CNN's web site, Monita Rajpal observed,

"Everywhere we go, everywhere we look, we are inundated with messages. We don't even have to think for ourselves. All we have to do is sit on our comfy couch and be told how to live our lives. From how to look, what to wear, what to eat, what our homes should look like, how to meet people, what to drive, practically every facet of our lives is taken care of. That is the power of advertising. . . . In this age of multiple mediums, advertising is everywhere— whether it's a pop-up campaign with people dancing at the train station (T-Mobile) that serves a multitude of platforms from television to the web, or a home-video-type commercial that is posted on YouTube. We may not have to think for ourselves as much but we do have to be more discriminating to decipher what is credible and what isn't. Bottom line though, advertising is a part of our existence. The good news is we're the ones with the power to choose."[4]

The impact of advertising is pervasive and insidious. We're like the proverbial "frog in a kettle." We don't even notice that we're slowly being boiled in the world's values and marinated with the taste for the pleasures of this world! These values have become instantly available to anyone with a computer or a smart phone. Internet access is pervasive in our culture and around the world. In fact, psychologists have recently identified an alarming trend of people who have become addicted to Internet activities. They call it Internet Addiction Disorder. Some of those who suffer from this problem have been hospitalized to break the addiction of constantly checking Facebook, Instagram, and all the other social media sites. I know what you're thinking, "Bless Ken's heart! He probably recently switched from cassette tapes to CD's. He just doesn't understand the modern world!" But please consider this: people at every age long for and desperately need to connect with others, and social media has become a primary measuring device of acceptance and self-esteem. In my view, it's much easier to develop a superficial relationship (often using a fake persona or at least filtering the facts) than spending the time and investing selfless commitment to develop genuine, lasting relationships. Postings on social media sites let people make an impression without the rigor of developing authentic relationship. And sadly, the messages posted online aren't always about puppies and cheesecakes. We hear stories of verbal abuse, bullying and negative, hurtful messages that are a steady diet of social media. People are being deeply hurt, and people are becoming social media addicts. That's the truth!

But wait . . . social media can promote healthy interaction with lifelong friends and family members. Online connections aren't all bad, and not everyone is addicted.

The flesh

Human nature buys the half-lies of advertising. Sure, the soft drink may taste good and the credit card may make buying more convenient, but the real promise of the ads goes straight to our hearts. We long for the acclaim, the power, and the popularity the ads promise. Human nature is the desire to be complete apart from God, to be "the master of our fate and the captain of our souls." As we strain and struggle to carve out our place in the world, we enjoy enough success and popularity to keep us hooked. Eventually, however, it's not enough. No matter how much success, pleasure, possessions, and prestige we gain, our hearts remain empty. The emptiness drives us to perform even more, to compulsively please people to win approval, and to compare ourselves to everyone around us. The intensified pursuit only leaves us exhausted and emptier than before.

Even the heights of beauty, applause, and wealth can't fill an empty heart. We all know people who seem to be beating the system. They're music producers, business tycoons, gorgeous models, and brilliant scholars. Everyone looks at them and marvels. Even these people, though, realize they aren't what they project to the outside world. In a famous article in *Vanity Fair*, Madonna confessed that every new song she released made her feel alive, but between them, she felt lost and alone. She told the reporter, "My drive in life is from this horrible fear of being mediocre. And that's always pushing me, pushing me. Because even though I've become Somebody. I still have to prove that Somebody. My struggle has never ended and it probably never will."[5]

Chris Evert, the professional tennis star, admitted that she struggled with her sense of inadequacies and used victories as a kind of medicine for her broken heart. The medicine, though, became addictive. She explained, "I had no idea who I was, or what I could be away from tennis. I was depressed and afraid because so much of my life had been defined by my being a tennis champion. I was completely lost. Winning made me feel like I was somebody. It made me feel pretty. It was like being hooked on a drug. I needed the wins, the applause, in order to have an identity."[6]

Tom Brady is one of the greatest NFL quarterbacks. He led his team, the Patriots, to three Super Bowl titles. He's a gifted athlete, he's married to a stunningly beautiful supermodel, he's incredibly handsome, and he makes millions in salary and endorsements—and his teammates love him. It would be hard to find anyone who has a more charmed life, yet in an interview with *60 Minutes*, Brady talked about the stress of fame. In spite of all the money and prestige, he admitted feeling confused and empty. He asked sadly, "How can I have three Super Bowl rings and still think there's something greater out there for me?" He had reached his highest goals and fulfilled every desire, but he complained, "God, there's got to be more than this!"

The interviewer asked, "What's the answer?"

Brady laughed. "I wish I knew. I love playing football, and I love being the quarterback for this team. But at the same time, there are a lot of other parts about me that I'm trying to find."[7]

If Tom Brady's prestige, possessions, power, and pleasure can't fill the emptiness in his life, we're foolish to think these things can fill the hole in our hearts. So, many of the blemishes on the canvas of our lives radiate from the influences of the world and the flesh, but there's another source that is in many ways the most destructive.

The devil

In his brilliant satire, *The Screwtape Letters*, C. S. Lewis said that Christians make one of two mistakes in their assumptions about Satan: "There are two equal and opposite errors into which our race can fall about the devils. One is to disbelieve in their existence. The other is to believe, and to feel an excessive and unhealthy interest in them. They themselves are equally pleased by both errors and hail a materialist or a magician with the same delight."[8]

The devil is a very real adversary, but God is far stronger and wiser. Satan's primary ploys are to use the world and our human nature in three ways: to tempt us, to deceive us, and to accuse us. To tempt us, he doesn't need to sweat! He uses the lure of advertising to entice us to pursue anything and everything other than God as the source of light and life. He deceives us with lies, half-lies, and misapplied truth. We realize that this special deception of Satan's is obvious in his temptation of Eve in the Garden: what he told her was *almost* true. The same is apparent in the temptations of Jesus. Satan used distorted truth in his attempt to entice the Son of God to sin. Quite often, we suffer the consequences of believing his lies and wonder, "How could I have been so blind? Why didn't I see this coming?" But Satan also is called "the accuser." When we sin, he whispers to us, "See, you're a loser! You call yourself a Christian, but God can't love someone like you!"

Satan doesn't have to look far for material to tempt, deceive, and accuse us. He has plenty of resources in the pervasive advertising, our incessant comparing of ourselves with others, and our flawed human nature that longs for things that can't satisfy.

Excuses and Resistance

The grace of God shatters these false conceptions of meaning and life. In the priceless love of Christ, we find living water that truly satisfies our thirst, light that illumines the darkness, and acceptance that calms our deepest fears. The problem, of course, is that we struggle to believe God's marvelous message. Even though we hear the truth of God's amazing love, we make excuses to turn away and go back to our pursuit of success, pleasure and approval. We long for authentic love, joy, and purpose, but we resist God and return to the empty well, hoping that this time we'll find what our hearts long for. This problem isn't new. God spoke through the prophet Jeremiah, "My people have committed two sins: They have forsaken me, the spring of living water, and have dug their own cisterns, broken cisterns that cannot hold water" (Jeremiah 2:13).

In the priceless love of Christ, we find living water that truly satisfies our thirst, light that illumines the darkness, and acceptance that calms our deepest fears.

Various myths motivate us to protect misguided "esteem-building" images. These myths, proclaimed over and over in our own thoughts and words, keep alive the doubts we have about ourselves, reinforcing pride and shame. Some of them are:

- "If I don't have enough money, possessions, or intelligence, I'm nobody."

- "If I'm not beautiful (handsome, thin, tall, athletic, strong), I won't be accepted."

- "If I say something stupid, no one will like me."

- "I come from a dysfunctional family, so I'm scarred for life."

- "I've been neglected (rejected, abused...), and I can never fully recover."

- "If I don't obey God perfectly, Jesus won't claim me as one of his."

- "If I commit that sin one more time, God is going to give up on me."

- "People desperately need me, but I'll only let them down."

- "I'm divorced, and I'll wear that condemning label the rest of my life."

What are your myths? What messages do you play over and over in your own mind that could be contributing to a discouraging sense of identity? Many of these myths are planted in you by Satan, the master of deceit. He doesn't want you to believe that you're "fearfully and wonderfully made" by the Master Artist. As long as the myths remain unchallenged, we stay stuck in negative thinking—the "voices within" seem completely normal. But when we recognize the myths, we have the opportunity to reject them and focus on the wonderful truths of our new identity and the promises of God!

You've Got to Be Kidding!

As we saw earlier, one of the most stirring stories in the Bible is about Moses. We often think of him as the great leader who pointed the way for his people to find the Promised Land. He certainly became a great leader, but we need to go back to the earlier part of the narrative to understand how he found that role. When he was a baby, the pharaoh planned to have all the Hebrew babies killed, but Moses' mother put him in a reed basket and floated him in the Nile River. The pharaoh's daughter found the basket and kept the child as her own. Moses grew up surrounded by unimaginable wealth and power.

At a critical moment, he discovered his identity as a Hebrew. When he saw an Egyptian taskmaster treat a Hebrew slave with cruelty, he murdered the man. He thought he was going to free God's people, but he had some lessons to learn! Now, God's people rejected him as an outsider, and the Egyptians rejected him as a Hebrew and a murderer. He was banished to the backside of the desert. It is easy to see that he didn't have a whole lot of room for bragging rights. There, as a poor shepherd, he learned the lessons of humility (Exodus 2:11-22).

When the time was right, God appeared to Moses in a burning bush and commanded him to be his instrument to free the slaves in Egypt. The arrogant, violent man from forty years before was no longer to be found. When God gave him his mission, Moses began to backpedal. In those years in the desert, he became keenly aware of his limitations. Listen to the conversation between God and his reluctant servant.

Aren't you thankful that when our human confidence is at an all-time low, God reminds us that he is faithful? The story isn't about us, but about his work in and through us. The Lord God didn't call Moses to do his special work because he was qualified, because he was experienced, because he was educated, or because he had special abilities. It was none of these! Moses was obsessed with self-conscious doubts and fears. In response to Moses' repeated declarations of reasons why God chose the wrong man, God answered with dramatic demonstrations. God asked Moses to throw down his rod, and it turned into a snake. God asked Moses to put his hand into his vest and take it out. It turned into leprosy (a certain death sentence at that time in history), and then it was clean when he repeated the exercise. Here is how the highlights of the conversation unfolded:

> God declares: "I've seen how miserable my people are in Egypt and I want you to get them out."
>
> Moses is surprised: "Who me? Why me? I'm nobody. The Egyptians won't listen to me. Besides, I'm afraid. Remember,

I killed one of them and they might still be looking for me."

God patiently responds: "The ones who wanted to kill you are all dead. Besides, I'll be with you."

Moses is confused: "The Israelites won't listen to me. They hate me because I grew up in Pharaoh's palace. Why should they trust me?"

God answers: "Tell them the God of your fathers—of Abraham, Isaac, and Jacob—sent you to them. I AM is sending you to them."

Moses is doubtful: "What if they don't believe me?"

God convinces him: "I'll help you perform miracles that will convince them."

Moses pleads: "But, Lord, I never did speak Hebrew very well, even when I lived there. And I haven't even conversed in Egyptian for forty years."

God corrects him: "Who made your mouth? I will help you speak and will tell you what to say."

Moses whines: "Oh, please, God. Send somebody else."

God has the final word: "Your brother Aaron, the priest, knows how to speak to both Israelites and Egyptians. He can talk for you. Now get ready and go meet Aaron; he's already on his way here to see you." (Paraphrased from Exodus 3-4.)

Talk about not being able to see the finished portrait! For forty years, Moses had assumed his life's mission was over, but the Master Artist was using those lonely years to prepare him for bigger things. God had a great commission for Moses: to assure that God's plan for salvation of mankind would continue. God had called the Hebrew people his people, those who would worship only him and from whom the

Savior of the world would come. The Hebrew people had to get back to the land that God had promised to Abraham, and God chose Moses to take them back. That commission was the greatest challenge Moses would ever receive—one with far-reaching, eternal consequences. God knew that Moses was capable of fulfilling it as long as he willingly placed himself on the eternal easel of the Master Artist.

The rest of the story is well known. God used Moses to call down ten plagues on the pharaoh and the Egyptians, so that finally, the slaves were set free. Then, when the Egyptian army came after them, God miraculously opened the Red Sea for the Hebrews to pass safely through, but the Egyptian army drowned. Moses led God's people to the gates of the Promised Land. Each one of us is also commissioned by God to do something with our lives. If we worry about our inadequacies and insecurities, we forget that we're fearfully and wonderfully made. We need to recognize the great lies we are fed every day that prevent us from realizing our God-given potential.

> **If we worry about our inadequacies and insecurities, we forget that we're fearfully and wonderfully made.**

Restoring the Masterpiece

In 1498, a twenty-three-year-old Florentine sculptor signed a unique contract. He agreed to complete in marble within one year, a statue of the Pieta (figures of Mary holding her crucified Son on her lap) to be placed in the Cathedral of Saint Peter's in Rome. In the contract he promised that the figure of Christ would be "of the size of a proper man" and the work would be done "for the price of 450 ducats of the papal mint." He had already done a number of sculptures, none of which attracted much attention.

As he began to chip away at the massive piece of marble, the young sculptor envisioned the dead Christ draped across his mother's lap, but his concept was different than most people expected. It would not be stark and grisly like many paintings of the scene. Instead, he planned to depict Christ as merely asleep—to suggest that he will rise again. The mother's left hand would express grief at her great loss, but also acceptance that her Son was crucified for the benefit of the world.

One year later, true to his word, the sculptor presented the completed statue. It immediately received acclaim. The figures were finished to a degree of refinement and subtlety that was unmatched at that time. For the first and perhaps the last time, the young man signed his name to his work, recognizing that it well could be his life's greatest endeavor. On the band that lay diagonally along the mother's breast, he carved in Latin: "Michelangelo Buonarroti the Florentine made it."

For nearly five hundred years, visitors to the chapel in Rome quietly, reverently, and contemplatively gazed at the magnificent Pieta. Then, one day in 1971, a deranged man invaded the chapel and savagely attacked the Pieta with a hammer, damaging the mother's face. He was arrested and carried away. All the pieces of the sculpture were collected from the floor and saved. Painstakingly, Vatican conservators restored the statue. Today, visitors can once again view the sculpture, now located behind bulletproof glass, sealed against the onslaught of any who would destroy the masterpiece.

Like the sculpture, we have been deeply marred, but God is restoring the masterpiece he has created. It begins in an instant, but the Artist paints his image on the canvas of our lives. He never gives up. He promises to complete the portrait. What remains unfinished in this life will be completed when we meet him face to face. For now, we can count on his promises and be confident in his protection as he continues the restoration process. We must courageously and intentionally embrace God's truth: we are, in fact, a masterpiece in the making, a portrait in progress, to the glory of God and our own good. That's the truth!

God is under no illusions about us. The writer to the Hebrews confronts us with this point: "Nothing in all creation is hidden from God's sight. Everything is uncovered and laid bare before the eyes of him to whom we must give account" (Hebrews 4:13). He knows our deepest secrets and our worst flaws, and he loves us still. Pastor and professor Henry Scougal observed, "For the excellency of a soul is to be measured by the object of its love."[9] We flawed, selfish human beings are the object of Christ's love, so his soul must be infinitely large and excellent! Blessed indeed!

Real love always involves sacrifice. Parents sacrifice for their children, spouses sacrifice for each other, soldiers fight and die for their country and each other, and friends sacrifice for the good of one another. Jesus lived in the beauty and glory of perfection in heaven. He needed nothing; he had everything imaginable. But he stepped out of the glory of heaven to bear the punishment we deserve, to take our place, and pay the price for our sins. If the measure of love is how much it gives, we realize Jesus' love is beyond comprehension because he gave it all for us.

Compensating for self-doubts is natural; cooperating with the Master Artist is supernatural. We have a choice: to see ourselves as hopelessly flawed or driven to prove ourselves, or in contrast, seeing ourselves as a portrait in progress. When we see ourselves through God's eyes, we're filled with anticipation of the finished masterpiece.

As we consider our flawed portraits, we need to be ruthlessly honest about our sins. Like the two brothers in Jesus' story of the prodigal, some of us have committed "younger brother sins" of adultery, addiction, lying, stealing, and other forms of blatant selfishness. Jesus died to pay for them all. But others of us have committed "elder brother sins" of self-righteousness, superiority, and pride that we "aren't like those people." Jesus died for those sins, too.

In his letter to the Ephesians, Paul describes us as hopelessly lost apart from God's loving intervention. We don't bargain with the holy King of the universe; we can't twist his arm by our good deeds. We come to him with empty hands and hungry hearts. We deserve God's righteous wrath, but we get something completely different. Paul explains:

> **We come to him with empty hands and hungry hearts. We deserve God's righteous wrath, but we get something completely different.**

> "But because of his great love for us, God, who is rich in mercy, made us alive with Christ even when we were dead in transgressions—it is by grace you have been saved. And God raised us up with Christ and seated us with him in the heavenly realms in Christ Jesus, in order that in the coming ages he might show the incomparable riches of his grace, expressed in his kindness to us in Christ Jesus" (Ephesians 2:4-7).

We may not want to admit it, but we're more sinful than we ever imagined, but because of Christ, we're more loved than we ever dared hope. The Bible tells us that Christ's sacrifice accomplished many things for us and in us. All our sins are completely forgiven, we are now "in Christ" by faith, clothed with his righteousness, and God has adopted us as his own. We belong to him, and he delights in us!

Juliana had been plagued for years by the critical, condemning, guilt-ridden "voices within." When she began to experience God's magnificent grace, the loving voice of God gradually became louder than those harsh voices. She began to believe—in the depths of her soul—that she was more valuable to God than the stars in the sky! For the first time in years, she felt loved, and God's amazing love gave her more joy and freedom than she ever imagined could be possible. Most of us realize it's not humanly possible to literally forget painful past circumstances. The good news is that we can choose what we do with the memories.

We will spend a lifetime diving deeper into the wonder of God's amazing grace. In the strength and love we find there, we'll find the courage to be honest about the flaws in our portrait, and we'll realize God is painting a new one for us. It's not about my failures and flaws, but about his favor. It's not about the *blemishes* in my life, but about his *blessings* in my life.

Consider this . . .

1. What are your favorite commercials? What is the surface promise for the product or service? What is the deeper promise of how it will give ultimate happiness and meaning? What are some reasons we believe these promises?

2. How does comparison poison our hearts and ruin relationships? Many people compare appearance, possessions, and positions. What do you naturally compare? How does it affect you when you're doing better than others? And when you're not?

3. Describe some specific ways Satan tempts, deceives, and accuses. Which of these is a problem for you? Explain your answer.

4. If God's love is so attractive, why do we make excuses and resist him? How would you identify your excuses? In what ways do you resist God's grace?

5. How does Christ sacrifice on the cross begin (or continue) to restore the masterpiece God is creating in you?

A prayer . . .

Oh Lord, I've believed so many lies and pursued so many empty promises! Thank you for your forgiveness and patience! Give me courage to take off the masks I've been wearing to impress people. Thank you that you accept me by your great grace. Today, I trust you to . . .

CHAPTER 3

The Artist's Touch

We should be astonished at the goodness of God, stunned that He should bother to call us by name, our mouths wide open at His love, bewildered that at this very moment we are standing on holy ground.
—**Brennan Manning**

At some point, we realize life isn't working. We've tried to impress people. It worked for a while, but eventually, they saw our flaws. We tried to prove ourselves by our accomplishments. Each rung on the ladder of success felt good for a moment, but we were left feeling empty, confused, and alone. Some of us give up in a moment of crisis; others endure a long, silent nightmare of hopelessness. We may have very different stories, but in a way, they're very similar: we realize we need God to give us love, security, and purpose. We need him to give us a new identity, to restore our marred image into his glorious likeness.

God doesn't just give us a rulebook to live by and wish list to hope for—he gives us himself. The strength of the relationship isn't our talents or performance; it's his strong and loving hands. In fact, Isaiah says that God is more attentive to us than a nursing mother to her baby:

> "Can a mother forget the baby at her breast
> and have no compassion on the child she has borne?

> Though she may forget,
> I will not forget you!
> See, I have engraved you on the palms of my hands"
> (Isaiah 49:15-16).

There's no easy way to do a hard thing. Being transformed and conformed to the image of Christ is a lifetime of good news and bad news. Christ Jesus himself learned obedience through suffering. We prefer the resurrection power of Christ without the fellowship of his suffering.

When you're lonely, you can pray, "Jesus, I belong to you, and I know you're with me whether I feel your presence or not." When you're afraid, you can pray, "Lord, I belong to you, and I know you understand what's going on even when I don't." When you're happy, you can pray, "Jesus, I belong to you, and I'm grateful for all you've done for me." And when you fantasize about escaping to an easier or more exciting life, you can pray, "Lord, I belong to you, and you've chosen for me to walk with you through some difficult times so my faith will grow stronger."

"I Am . . ."

Throughout the pages of the Bible, God shouts wonderful truths about our new identity, and he whispers to convince us these things are really true. In a beautiful psalm about God's omniscience, omnipresence, and omnipotence, King David reflects also on God's attention to detail. God's brilliance in creating each of us, he asserts, is more wonderful than we can imagine. David wrote:

> "For you created my inmost being;
>   you knit me together in my mother's womb.
> I praise you because I am fearfully and wonderfully made;
>   your works are wonderful,

I know that full well.
My frame was not hidden from you
    when I was made in the secret place,
    when I was woven together in the depths of the earth.
Your eyes saw my unformed body;
    all the days ordained for me were written in your book
    before one of them came to be.
How precious to me are your thoughts, God!
    How vast is the sum of them!
Were I to count them,
    they would outnumber the grains of sand—
    when I awake, I am still with you" (Psalm 139:13-18).

Do you believe you are wonderfully handcrafted by the God of the universe? When we realize that God, the Master Artist, has fashioned our appearance, talents, and personality, we see ourselves through his eyes! God's creativity becomes precious to us, and we thank him for making us just like we are—warts, freckles, strange hair, odd sense of humor, innate caution, uncommon courage, and all!

We need new ammunition in our fight against the world's messages, our human nature's inclination to pride and shame, and the enemy's schemes to convince us we're unworthy and undeserving scum. This ammunition is a list of wonderful, inspiring "I am" statements. Let all of them sink into your soul, and then pick one that has special meaning to you.

> **Do you believe you are wonderfully handcrafted by the God of the universe?**

Even though it may seem too good to be true, here's a list of God's truths you can claim as your own:

- I am loved. (1 John 3:3)
- I am forgiven. (Colossians 3:13)
- I am accepted. (Ephesians 1:6)
- I am adopted as a child of God. (John 1:12, Romans 8:15)
- I am Jesus' friend. (John 15:14)
- I am a joint heir with Jesus, sharing his inheritance with him. (Romans 8:17)
- I am united with God and one spirit with him. (1 Corinthians 6:17)
- I am a temple of God. The Holy Spirit lives in me. (1 Corinthians 6:19)
- I am a member of Christ's body. (1 Corinthians 12:27)
- I am redeemed, purchased by Christ's blood. (Colossians 1:14)
- I am complete in Jesus Christ. (Colossians 2:10)
- I am free from condemnation. (Romans 8:1)
- I am a new creation in Christ. (2 Corinthians 5:17)
- I am chosen of God, holy and dearly loved. (Colossians 3:12)
- I am established, anointed, and sealed by God. (2 Corinthians 1:21)

- I do not have a spirit of fear, but of love, power, and a sound mind. (2 Timothy 1:7)
- I am God's co-worker. (2 Corinthians 6:1)
- I am seated in heavenly places with Christ. (Ephesians 2:6)
- I am light and salt. (Matthew 5:13-16)
- I am chosen to bear fruit. (John 15:16)
- I am one of God's living stones, being built up in Christ as a spiritual house. (1 Peter 2:5)
- I am the recipient of exceedingly great and precious promises by God by which I share his nature. (2 Peter 1:4)
- I am always in the presence of God because he never leaves me. (Hebrews 13:5)

Because of Christ, the Master Artist, you have:

- a love so vast that it can never fully be grasped,
- a life that can never die,
- a righteousness that can never be tarnished,
- a peace that can never be understood,
- a rest that can never be disturbed,
- a joy that can never be diminished,
- a hope that can never be disappointed,
- a glory that can never be clouded,

- a light that can never be darkened,
- a strength that can never be weakened,
- a purity that can never be defiled,
- a beauty that can never be marred,
- a wisdom that can never be baffled, and
- resources that can never be exhausted.[10]

Did you rush through all those "I am" statements and spiritual blessings? There are so many it's easy to let our minds drift. Go back and read them again. Let two or three of them sink deep into your mind and heart. Yes, they're all true, and one might seem to be particularly meaningful to you!

The Tension of Timing

If we're honest, the glorious truths about our identity thrill us, but they may also confuse us. We may ask, "If these things are true, why don't I feel them more deeply? Why don't I live my life according to them more fully?" Great questions!

The answer is that we live in the tension between the "already" and the "not yet."

The answer is that we live in the tension between the "already" and the "not yet." The Bible tells us that the blessings of being God's children are ours today, but the complete and unfettered enjoyment of them won't happen in this life. For example, in Romans 8, Paul says that we have already been adopted by God (verses 15-16), but only a few verses later, he says that we "groan inwardly as we wait eagerly for our adoption . . . the redemption of our bodies" (verse 23). Similarly, Paul assures us that our bodies are "temples of the Holy Spirit" (1 Corinthians 6:19), but the Spirit has been given to us as "a deposit" or "down payment" (Ephesians 1:13-14) on the full experience of the Spirit that will come in the new heaven and new earth. New Testament scholar N. T. Wright teaches that the kingdom of God was *inaugurated* at the death, resurrection, and ascension of Christ, but it will be fully *consummated* when Jesus comes back physically to rule on earth.

What does this mean for us? It means we can expect the painting to be in progress during our lifetimes. All the truths about our new identity are true—thank God they are! But our experience of them will be tarnished by sin and battered by the world, the flesh, and the devil until we see Jesus face to face. In some ways our life's journey is like the stretches of highways throughout our country, you don't have to travel far before you find road signs warning about potential danger because the road is perpetually "Under Construction." In the same way, God is still working on us!

Too Far to Go?

Many people sit in church every Sunday and listen to the wonderful message of grace and their new identity in Christ, but they simply can't imagine experiencing God's love like the pastor suggests. They assume, "I'm too flawed." "You don't know what I've done." "All this stuff about a new identity may be true for other people, but not me. I have way too far to go to ever experience God like that."

That's the enemy's voice they're hearing and repeating. It's certainly not God's message to them! When we read the Bible, we realize God takes great delight in showering his love on the most flawed men and women he could find. The "heroes" of the Bible are invariably those who committed the biggest sins or were voted by family and friends as the "most unlikely to succeed," but they found forgiveness and a new purpose in God's loving arms.

- Abraham was "the father of our faith," but he lied to save his skin and doubted God many times.

- Moses' pride led to a violent outburst that killed an Egyptian. Then, after forty years in the desert, his lack of confidence produced sinful doubt. Still, God used him to dramatically lead his people out of slavery to the edge of the Promised Land.

- Rahab was a prostitute, but she protected the Israelites who came to her city to plan their attack. She is listed in the lineage of Jesus Christ.

- Gideon was timid and fearful. God went to unusual measures to convince him to take action to defend the nation.

- David was a great warrior and king, but he committed adultery and murder.

- Peter boasted that he would be faithful to Jesus even if everyone else ran away, but he denied even knowing Jesus to three unassuming people. His arrogance was shattered, which made him a prime candidate to lead the early church.

- We often shake our heads at Thomas' doubts, but when Jesus appeared to him and gave him evidence, Thomas became one of the greatest missionaries of all time.

- Paul was determined to wipe Christians off the face of the earth, but an encounter with the risen Christ revolutionized his heart and changed his direction.

- Jeremiah claimed his youth and inexperience as an excuse for not trusting God.

God adds us to this list. All of us are individually fashioned by God's predetermined plan to fulfill His purpose . . . but not without a keen awareness of our inabilities, insecurities and inadequacies. Do you feel unqualified, deeply flawed, full of doubts, insecure, inadequate, and inferior? If you do, you're the perfect candidate for the grace of God! It's people like us who can gladly embrace God's love, forgiveness, power, and purpose. You will be appropriately stunned by your new identity that isn't earned. You'll be convinced it's a gift from God.

This isn't just an academic theory or a psychological concept. The love of God transforms people! I've seen countless men and women move from radical insecurity to genuine liberation. Some suffered abuse or abandonment, and many had been haunted by past sins. When I met them, many of them said they were coming to me as their last hope. Most had given up on ever regaining their identity in Christ. As I pointed them to the heart of Jesus, they thought God's love was too good to be true. I assured them it's absolutely true, and Jesus proved his love in the most dramatic possible way—by going to the cross to pay the ultimate price to demonstrate his affection for us! Slowly, these men and women lowered their defenses and let Jesus touch their deepest wounds and biggest fears. Joy began to replace depression; hope took the place of despair; and love crowded out their anger. As the love of God tenderized their hearts and molded their character, they began to reflect the nature of Jesus Christ. They loved the unlovely, forgave those who betrayed them, and cared for those who had been overlooked. The glory of God shined through them! It was a beautiful thing to see.

As long as we cling to the false hope of earning our status by our performance, our hands won't be open to receive God's amazing grace. Sometimes, God has to take us to the limit of ourselves so we'll finally reach out to him. This pattern for making a masterpiece out of a mess is amazingly clear in the stories of the scripture—and in the lives of men and women today.

Ron Ney was a successful high school and college athlete who continued his love for sports as a coach for college and NFL teams. His college assignments included UCLA, and his professional career included coaching for the New York Jets and the San Diego Chargers, where he was the General Manager.

During the height of his success, he had a wonderful wife and family, an enviable income, was respected in the community, and seldom experienced any major distractions from a string of unbroken successes.

Ron's wife took her relationship with the Lord Jesus very seriously. He was confident of her love, but because of his packed schedule, he didn't invest a lot of focused time on their marriage. His career was the most important thing in his life; it required enormous commitment.

As he approached retirement, Ron's life began to unravel. By this time, he was on the staff of the New York Jets. He thought things were going well, but the GM told him they were "going in a different direction," and they let him go. He didn't consider this to be a major problem. He was confident that another team would offer him a position on their coaching staff. In the meantime, he played a little golf and got some rest.

He contacted the front offices of football teams and made himself available. They all acknowledged his value and offered to do what they could to find him another position. What he thought would be a matter of weeks turned into months . . . and then years.

During this agonizing period, Ron began to experience a flood of self-critical doubts and life-altering fears. He lost his appetite, and for a short time, he lost all motivation for life and living. Ron thought he was at the bottom, but he soon suffered another blow: his father died. The loss was devastating. His dad had always been his confidant.

When Ron called me for counseling, he was filled with hopelessness, broken in spirit, and financially stressed. He needed a job, but his football career was at a dead-end. He took a job shuttling and supervising mentally handicapped young people around town as they washed windows at various businesses. He even took a job as a janitor, cleaning restrooms. He had literally gone from the peak of success to the valley of despair, from general manager to garbage manager, from press-box windows to washing windows.

Ron knew what it meant to be a Christian, but he was only superficially interested in spiritual things. He sometimes attended church during the off-season, but he wasn't especially interested in his spiritual development.

During the course of counseling, Ron got on his knees in my office and asked Jesus Christ to forgive him of his sins and become his Savior. It wasn't long before he began to see life through the filters of faith. He acknowledged that God had allowed much of his suffering in order to bring him to his knees. Then his life began to change. He returned to professional football and had many more successful years in his career. He is now enjoying his retirement.

When Ron began to see himself as God's work of art and experienced the grace of Jesus Christ, everything changed. He soon had a renewed appreciation and love for his wife, and he had a new appreciation for what's really important in life. He has a passion to tell others of Jesus Christ. As he reviews the long, disturbing chapter of his life, he understands that God used those difficulties to work deeply in his heart. He now sees himself as a masterpiece in the making, a portrait in progress, and he's taking on the characteristics of Christ, conforming to his image. With a radiant smile, Ron declares today, "Having the right foundation is critical in every area of life. But it's absolutely essential in being able to see yourself as a masterpiece in the making, especially when so many circumstances are outside of our control."

Training Camp

I'm appropriately proud of my family for the commitment and sacrifices they made serving our country in the military. My brother Larry served in the Army for over twenty years. He was a paratrooper in the Army Special Forces and received multiple honors/medals as a Viet Nam veteran. Colonel Ted Nichols, my younger brother, served as an Army Chaplain for twenty-six years and impacted many men for Christ during the Desert Storm campaign. My dad served in World War II as a Marine.

When I was a child I watched movies of soldiers jumping out of planes and drifting to the ground in parachutes. I thought that would be exciting! I was eighteen years old when I proudly followed my brother's example and arrived at the U.S. Army Paratrooper Training Camp, determined to become the best of the army elite.

Although I didn't know it at the time, the drill sergeant's vocational obsession for the first week of training was to break us down. He let us know that we couldn't do anything right. We paid for our mistakes by doing hundreds of push-ups. We began each day by standing at attention by our beds while the sergeant went down the line and tossed a silver dollar onto each bunk bed. If the bed wasn't made tightly so the coin bounced high enough for him to catch it (he didn't seem to try very hard sometimes), he would rip the covers off the bunk and demand that we make it right—just as soon as we had completed the grueling push-ups. By the second day, nearly everyone experienced intense fear from the mental harassment and emotional intimidation.

Nobody... I mean... *nobody* joins the army airborne who doesn't already have considerable self-confidence in his physical abilities. It's not an assignment for the faint of heart.

I'll never forget when I messed up a practice jump from the 250 foot training tower. Three sergeants ordered me to approach. I knew how excited they were to use me as a demonstration to the rest of the class.

"Drop and do fifty push-ups!"

"Had enough, soldier?"

"No, Sir!" I bellowed back at him. (I lied, but it's part of the bravado they instill.) I mean... I couldn't hardly say, "Hey, thanks for asking. I'm a bit exhausted."

"Do fifty more then!"

Well, that was over 50 years ago, and I'm just curious! I want to conduct a brief reader survey. How many of you believe that at this stage of my life I can still do 50 push-ups? Come on now; raise your hands. Do you really believe I can? You will find the answer on the last page of the book. Now wait! Don't even think of looking ahead!

After just a few days, we were stripped of all of our confidence and the masks of bravado we'd been wearing to impress others. The image we had projected to hide our inner insecurities was totally dismantled. Suddenly, we were exposed. We were reduced to the basics. We had no place to hide... no impressive image.

The sergeant confronted us with incredible challenges that would make it impossible for us to succeed. His goal was for us to leave the training grounds totally humiliated. But we didn't understand that the immense pressure was actually a prerequisite to rebuild us and reshape our identity. The suffering we endured was intended to instill courage, confidence, and camaraderie in all who survived training camp. The sergeant knew that these traits were critical ingredients in the making of a paratrooper. He was determined to "create" the kind of soldier that would have that rare blend of confidence and humility—especially, like my brothers, when risking their lives in combat.

Today, as I look back at that thoroughly humiliating, exhausting and exhilarating training, I see the parallel in my Christian experience. I realize that a prerequisite to developing a strong, healthy, and biblical sense of identity is a willingness to identify elements of my false identity and replace them with the new one. It's not simple or easy. In paratrooper training and spiritual training, we often have to be brought to the end of our own resources before we're willing to be rebuilt.

> **If we understand God's purposes, times of suffering can be viewed as opportunities, not obstacles, as blessings rather than blemishes on our portrait.**

God lovingly puts us in situations that bring us to the limits of our abilities and confidence. If we understand God's purposes, times of suffering can be viewed as opportunities, not obstacles, as blessings rather than blemishes on our portrait. In his book, *The Awakened Heart*, Gerald May wrote,

"I am sure God wants us to be whole and healthy in every way possible, but love neither depends upon these things nor ends with them. In fact, blessings sometimes come through brokenness that could never come in any other way. In reflecting on my own life, I have to conclude that grace has come through me more powerfully sometimes when I have been very dysfunctional and maladjusted. Love transcends all possible adjustments and continually invites us through and beyond them."[11]

Consider this . . .

1. What difference does it make (or might it make if you choose to believe it) for you to be convinced—in good times and bad—that you belong to God?

2. Pick two of the "I am" statements and two of the "I have" statements that are most meaningful to you. How do these comfort you? How do they challenge you to live more confidently and boldly?

3. All of us have some sense of resistance to the extravagance of God's amazing love and our new identity. How would you define and describe your resistance? How will you overcome it?

4. How does the realization that we live in the tension between the "already" and the "not yet" give you perspective, peace, and confidence?

5. How has God used difficulties, conflicts, and disappointments to bring you to an end of yourself?

6. What is God's loving purpose for allowing these painful events in our lives? What's the difference between godly brokenness and depression?

A prayer . . .

Oh Jesus, can these things really be true? I want to let the truth of your love and grace sink deep into my heart. The truths about my identity that mean the most to me are . . . . Today, I want to reflect your love, courage, kindness, and strength in these situations:

CHAPTER 4

A New Image Takes Shape

If Christ lives in us, controlling our personalities, we will leave glorious marks on the lives we touch. Not because of our lovely characters, but because of his.

—**Eugenia Price**

A few years ago, some friends visited Jackson Hole, Wyoming, on a trip to Yellowstone and the Grand Tetons. On a Saturday in the town square, city officials sponsored a "quick draw" contest. About thirty famous (and not so famous) Western artist set up their easels and paint boxes. They were given an hour to complete their work of art. My friends wandered around looking at the first brush strokes of several artists, but they decided to spend the rest of the hour watching a particular man. For most of the hour, he used broad strokes to lay down background colors. Gradually, the vertical elements of trees took shape. With only a few minutes to go, it looked like he was hopelessly behind schedule. His canvas was a blurry mass of seemingly disconnected colors. Then, the artist used an array of brushes to apply shades of brown and black paint. Almost like magic, a majestic moose appeared in the center of his painting! With a few more strokes, tree trunks, limbs, and foreground foliage came into view. As the announcer called "Time's up!" he stepped back from his finished work. It was stunningly beautiful!

In a similar way, our lives are the canvas on which the Master Artist paints a beautiful image. For a while, it may appear that not much is happening. It may, in fact, look like a bunch of disconnected blobs of paint. But the Master knows what he's doing. Sooner or later, the image takes shape. We're no longer manipulated by shame or inflated by foolish pride. We have a sense of humility and confidence. We're no longer resentful because our lives haven't turned out the way we planned. Instead, we realize God is using all the heartaches to deepen our dependence on him and shape our character. We're no longer bitter at those who have hurt us. The magnificent love and forgiveness of God floods our hearts and overflows in kindness toward those who have wronged us. We're not shackled to our failures and wounds of the past, and we're not afraid of the future. We're no longer hopeless; we realize we're connected to the ultimate source of hope—God's gracious love, wisdom, and acceptance.

As we increasingly listen to God's grace-filled message instead of the negative ones from our past or from our enemy, God gradually transforms us to become more and more like Jesus. When Moses met God at the burning bush, the radiance of God's presence changed Moses' appearance—everyone noticed! In fact, the glow of his face was so intense that he had to wear a veil to cover the glory. Paul looks back at that event and connects it to our heartfelt, transforming encounter with the living God. He explained to the Corinthians: "But whenever anyone turns to the Lord, the veil is taken away. Now the Lord is the Spirit, and where the Spirit of the Lord is, there is freedom. And we all, who with unveiled faces contemplate the Lord's glory, are being transformed into his image with ever-increasing glory, which comes from the Lord, who is the Spirit" (2 Corinthians 3:16-18).

How does the inner change happen so that our attitudes and actions reflect Christ? It's by focusing our minds and hearts on Christ's character and letting the wonder of his grace sink deep into us. We only become kind when we realize how incredibly kind he is, even to those who rejected him. We only become patient when we begin to grasp the depths of his patience with people who are slow to understand—people like you and me. We only become humble when our hearts are overwhelmed that the King of All became a human being to connect with us, and even more, that he suffered and died to pay a price we couldn't pay. We only care about the things God cares about when we are convinced that only God and his purposes make all the difference.

In this process, we become increasingly aware of the games we've been playing to impress people and carve out a place in the world. Hidden motives come into the light of God's truth, and we find more forgiveness than we ever imagined. Because we're loved, we're not afraid of being exposed to the one who loves us.

Transformation is never easy or smooth. For Moses, doubts had to be replaced by faith in God's wisdom and power. In the wilderness as he led God's people, he often demonstrated remarkable courage in the face of opposition, but occasionally, his doubts got the best of him. Through it all, God assured Moses by accompanying him and the Israelites on their journey. During the day, God traveled with them in a visible cloud, and at night, his presence was apparent in a pillar of fire. The amazing story is only partly about Moses; even more, it's about the astounding love, patience, and purposes of Moses' God.

God's Part, Our Part

Some believers make a wrong assumption about the Christian life. They think grace is a ticket to heaven, and they believe they're left to their own wisdom and strength to try to live in the way God wants them to live. Many of them think of God only on Sunday morning and when they experience calamities. They see God as a filling station they visit occasionally when they need some spiritual fuel.

That's not the picture the Bible paints of the abundant life! When we realize we belong to God, we understand it's a constant relationship. We're with him all day every day, and we trust him for wisdom and strength every moment. We don't drive in to a filling station from time to time. We are "in Christ" and his Spirit lives in us as a constant presence.

We don't obey to be blessed; we obey because we're blessed!

We've talked about God as the Master Artist, but paradoxically, he has given us a role to play in shaping the picture of our lives. Our obedience isn't a bargaining chip to get God to bless us; it's a response of a grateful child to a loving, wise parent. We don't obey *to be* blessed; we obey *because* we're blessed!

In Paul's letter to the Philippians, he describes the sacrifice of Christ in one of the most moving and beautiful passages in the Bible. He explains that Jesus stepped out of the glory of heaven to become a human being and die in our place. God honored him by raising him from the dead and seating him at his right hand in heaven. Paul then turns to us, the readers, and says, "Therefore, my dear friends, as you have always obeyed—not only in my presence, but now much more in my absence—continue to work out your salvation with fear and trembling, for it is God who works in you to will and to act in order to fulfill his good purpose" (Philippians 2:12-13).

As God paints our new image and identity, we aren't passive. God has given us the dignity of being his partners. As God's Spirit is at work in us to change us, equip us, direct us, and motivate us, we respond in glad obedience like a dearly loved child longs to please her parents. When our hearts are full and overflowing with God's love, we're no longer so self-absorbed. We realize: It's not about me; it's about him! God is at work in the depths of our hearts—our self-concept and our motivations—to transform us so that we reflect his love, kindness, wisdom and strength to a watching world. Peter put it like this: "But you are a chosen people, a royal priesthood, a holy nation, God's special possession, that you may declare the praises of him who called you out of darkness into his wonderful light" (1 Peter 2:9).

The portrait takes shape in tens of thousands of brush strokes. God's part is to illumine our minds to understand the Scriptures, to whisper assurance and correction to our hearts, and produce the fruit of love, joy, peace, patience, kindness, faithfulness, gentleness, and self-control—and to use us to touch the lives of those around us. Our part is to respond to the truth with a heart of faith, to listen to the Spirit's voice, and courageously act in ways that honor God in everything we do.

Our response to God always goes back to Christ's sacrifice for us. We obey because he first obeyed the Father to the point of death. After chapters of explaining God's magnificent grace to his readers, Paul gave this direction: "Follow God's example, therefore, as dearly loved children and walk in the way of love, just as Christ loved us and gave himself up for us as a fragrant offering and sacrifice to God" (Ephesians 5:1-2). We love because he loved us first, we obey because he obeyed first, and we reach out to others because he first reached out to us. That's the beauty and power of a life rooted in a new identity in Christ.

Choices

To illustrate how we can reflect and demonstrate God's image in our lives, Paul uses the metaphor of changing clothes:

> "You were taught, with regard to your former way of life, to put off your old self, which is being corrupted by its deceitful desires; to be made new in the attitude of your minds; and to put on the new self, created to be like God in true righteousness and holiness" (Ephesians 4:22-24).

When we change clothes, we first recognize the ones we're wearing are dirty or wrinkled or inappropriate for an event we plan to attend. We conclude a change needs to be made, so we unbutton, unzip, and take off the unwanted clothes. Then, (perhaps after taking a shower), we go to the closet and choose the clothes we want to wear. In the reverse of taking off the unwanted clothes, we pull on, button up, and zip everything into place. All of these things have become instinctual to us because we do it at least a couple of times every day of our lives.

Paul says we do the same thing when we exchange our "old self" for our "new self." The old self is our sinful, selfish desires fueled by the world, the flesh, and the devil. Our new self is our new status, our new identity as children of the King. We don't change just by sitting in our old clothes and hoping something magical will happen. We cooperate with the Spirit of God to "change clothes." We notice our destructive habits, resentment, greed, sexual drift, gossip, lies, and any other attitudes and behavior that don't reflect the nature of God. We don't sit and examine them forever. When we see them, we grab them, put them aside, and put on the godly alternative. We make dozens of choices each day. The Bible calls this process "repentance." We turn from a destructive, selfish kind of behavior and attitude to those that please God. In this passage, Paul gives several practical examples of "putting off" and "putting on":

- Put off falsehood and speak truthfully (verse 25).

- Be appropriately angry at injustice, but don't let anger fester in your soul (verses 26-27).

- Don't steal, but work and give to those in need (verse 28).

- Don't speak destructively, but use your words constructively (verses 29-30).

- Don't let bitterness ruin your heart and relationships, but be kind and forgiving, just as Christ has been kind and forgiving to you (verses 31-32).

These are just a few representative samples of the choices we can make every day. At dozens of points in an average day, we have the choice: to wallow in our old clothes or take them off and put on new ones. Our new identity shapes our responses in every relationship. In a parallel passage, Paul tells us, "Therefore, as God's chosen people, holy and dearly loved, clothe yourselves with compassion, kindness, humility, gentleness and patience" (Colossians 3:12). If we read the Bible with open eyes, we'll see countless passages that show how our new identity shapes every aspect of our lives.

Our new identity becomes completely ours the instant we trust Christ as our Savior, but realizing and experiencing the impact of that status is a long, gradual process. When we have children, we may not notice how they've grown from one day to the next, but if we put a series of pictures on the wall at one-year intervals, we'll see a dramatic transformation. In the same way, we may not notice how God is changing us from the inside out, but over time, those who are watching us will be able to see the difference.

> We may not notice how God is changing us from the inside out, but over time, those who are watching us will be able to see the difference.

As you see your life's portrait taking shape, be both diligent and patient. Be tenacious in pursuing God, being honest when he shows you some dirty clothes in your life, and trusting in his forgiveness and power to transform you as you make choices to put on your new self. And be patient with the process. Human beings grow through stages of childhood, adolescence, and adulthood, often becoming parents and grandparents. Spiritually, we also grow in stages. Sometimes, growth spurts happen quickly, but more often, it's very gradual.

Growth Principles

Timeless principles to give direction for personal growth have been emphasized for generations. They apply in every aspect of life. They're not the product of some philosopher . . . God thought of them first.

Cultivate a positive attitude

When you know where you want to go, you can be assured "that in all things God works for the good of those who love him, who have been called according to his purpose" (Romans 8:28). Being called "according to his purpose" means that God knew you were going to be his long before you were born. God wants you to succeed. There are only two requirements: love God and be sure you have surrendered to his "purpose." By God's grace and his promised provision, commit yourself to cooperate with God as he brushes a positive, biblical attitude onto the canvas of your portrait.

Define your purpose

Paul wrote, "Forgetting what is behind and straining toward what is ahead, press on toward the goal to win the prize for which God has called you" (Philippians 3:13-14). Turn off the old recordings of past failure or discouragement that distort your opinion of yourself, your abilities, and your confidence in God. Press on toward your goal. Our purpose in life is to honor Christ and reflect his love, wisdom, and strength to those around us. When we understand our ultimate purpose in life, we're free to fulfill it with enthusiasm and satisfaction.

Go the extra mile

Jesus told his followers, "If someone forces you to go one mile, go with him two miles" (Matthew 5:41). No one has ever achieved his goal without being willing to do more than what was expected of him. Cultivating a selfless attitude and going beyond what's expected is one of the features of our new identity. In the midst of a self-dominated society, selflessness is a remarkable (and rare) personal trait.

Live enthusiastically

A passion for life builds your self-esteem, and it delights those whose lives you touch. Solomon reminds us: "Whatever your hand finds to do, do it with all your might" (Ecclesiastes 9:10). The word "enthusiasm" in Greek is a combination of two words: *en* meaning "in," and *theos* meaning "God." Enthusiasm means being inspired by God.

Get Involved, Stay Involved

The writer to the Hebrews wrote, "Let us not give up meeting together, as some are in the habit of doing, but let us encourage one another" (Hebrews 10:25). We need the encouragement and input of people we trust. We are told in Scripture to pray for one another, encourage one another daily, rejoice together, and confess our faults to one another. We need the strength of others to help us achieve our purposes. It's in giving that I gain. It's in serving that I grow. It's in caring for others that I'm nurtured.

It's in giving that I gain. It's in serving that I grow. It's in caring for others that I'm nurtured.

When I deal with men and women in counseling who are depressed, I generally encourage them to begin caring for the needs of others. It is amazing what happens to us when we change the focus from our deficits to the needs of others.

Maintain physical health

Paul explained, "Do you not know that your body is a temple of the Holy Spirit, who is in you, whom you have received from God? Therefore honor God with your body" (1 Corinthians 6:19-20). Taking care of our bodies is part of being good spiritual stewards. Many physical problems are caused by stress, but exercise, sleep, and a good diet can greatly reduce levels of stress. The discipline required to take care of yourself physically promotes discipline in every area of your life. Good stewardship of your body pays remarkable dividends.

Think accurately

Paul instructed, "Do not conform any longer to the pattern of this world, but be transformed by the renewing of your mind. Then you will be able to test and approve what God's will is—his good, pleasing and perfect will" (Romans 12:1). You renew your mind by learning—more about your goal or learn more about your God. You can't think accurately unless you know the truth. The Bible tells us what we should think about and warns us to avoid certain thoughts (2 Corinthians 10:4-5). The more our mind, imagination, and thoughts are conformed to the mind of Christ, the more our behavior reflects his image.

Maintain self-discipline

Paul advises, "Run in such a way as to get the prize. Everyone who competes in the games goes into strict training. They do it to get a crown that will not last; but we do it to get a crown that will last forever. Therefore I do not run like a man running aimlessly; I do not fight like a man beating the air. No, I beat my body and make it my slave so that after I have preached to others, I myself will not be disqualified for the prize" (1 Corinthians 9:24-27). Self-discipline is a minute-by-minute exercise. The evil one is looking for an opening to exploit.

Keep the faith

"The Lord your God has given you the land. Go up and take possession of it as the Lord, the God of your fathers, told you. Do not be afraid; do not be discouraged" (Deuteronomy 1:21). Sometimes it's necessary to give ourselves pep talks when we feel discouraged. Try it! True faith shines brightest on the face of believers when they are facing the unknown or things that are outside their control.

Learn from defeat

Solomon wrote, "For though a righteous man falls seven times, he rises again" (Proverbs 24:16). Others will forget your defeats more quickly than you will. Don't dwell on them—learn from them.

Forgiveness: A Benchmark of Growth

One of the primary marks of a portrait painted by the Master is the beauty and power of forgiveness. On the other hand, as a counselor and pastor, I've witnessed the destructive consequences of an unforgiving spirit. Author Philip Yancey remarked that forgiveness is "the unnatural act." Everything in us cries out for revenge, but instead, forgiveness requires that we endure the painful offense and let the offender go free. One of the most destructive factors that erodes self-esteem is the unwillingness to forgive those who have hurt us. And one of the most powerful factors that deepens our sense of security in God's love is the ability to receive and give forgiveness. Let me put it this way: To the extent we experience and express God's forgiveness, to that extent we will be free to be the people God has called us to be.

We often make one of two mistakes: we forgive too quickly (without being honest about the depth of the hurt we've experienced) or too late (harboring resentment that leads to the poison of bitterness). Make no mistake: the portrait God is painting of your life necessarily involves the deep, rich colors of forgiveness. It's his nature, and he wants to impart that nature to us, too.

Forgiveness is one of the core features of the heart of God. For God so loved the world—he forgave us of our sins. From cover to cover the Bible emphasizes the importance of giving and receiving forgiveness. Forgiveness is essential in our portrait in progress.

> **Forgiveness isn't to free those who hurt you, but to free you from the hurt.**

The cycle of forgiveness often has to start with forgiving yourself. My daughter Kara expresses this concept in this special way: Forgiveness isn't to free those who hurt you, but to free you from the hurt.

Why is forgiving so hard? Because we tend to believe certain myths about giving and receiving forgiveness. Somehow, like bad genes, sincere but misguided notions get passed down from one generation to another. These misguided concepts are similar to the not-so-biblical but very familiar statement: "God helps those who help themselves." It seems right and is certainly familiar, but it's a misconception.

The most prevalent myths about forgiveness could be labeled:

- The hypocrite myth: "I can't forgive her yet because I don't feel like it, and I don't want to be a hypocrite."

- The unforgivable myth: "What he did to me is so awful that it's unforgivable."

- The memory myth: "I'll never forget the hurt of what she did to me, so I can't forgive her."

- The revenge myth: "I can't forgive him until I get even. When I'm deeply wounded by someone, it's only fair that he should also suffer—at least as much as I've suffered."

- The restoration myth: "I'll never be the same or regain what I've lost. The wounds are too deep."

- The trust and reconciliation myth: "Biblical forgiveness requires that I trust the person who hurt me, and reconcile even if he doesn't change."

Some people truly believe these myths when they're responding to emotional wounds. Pain makes it difficult to see God's truth clearly, and we become vulnerable to misconceptions of genuine forgiveness.[12]

Our capacity and motivation to forgive others comes out of our experience of God's forgiveness for our sins. When Peter asked how many times we should forgive, he thought he was being generous by suggesting seven times. Jesus answered, "seventy times seven"—in other words, an unlimited number of offenses. Then Jesus told a parable about a servant who owed the king billions of dollars. For the debt to be that huge, he had to have been the king's accountant. When the servant couldn't repay the debt, he fell at the king's feet and asked for more time. The king's heart was moved with compassion, so he completely forgave the whole debt! The story, though, doesn't end there. This servant left the king's palace and found a man who owed him a few hundred dollars. When the man couldn't repay him, he grabbed him, choked him, and had him thrown into debtors' prison. When the king found out, he was furious. He had the servant brought back, and he told him, "You wicked servant. I canceled all that debt of yours because you begged me to. Shouldn't you have had mercy on your fellow servant just as I had on you?" (Matthew 18: 32-33)

The answer to the question is, of course, yes, he should have given mercy because he had received so much mercy. In the same way, we are to forgive those who have hurt us "just as God in Christ has forgiven" us (Colossians 3:13).

Some people "have their consciences screwed on too loose"; that is, they don't feel very guilty when they do bad things. But many others "have their consciences screwed on too tight"; they feel terribly guilty and have difficulty experiencing God's forgiveness. For those in the "too tight" camp, let me offer this analogy: Years ago, I was picked up for driving a friend's car, but his license renewal was past due. When a policeman pulled me over, I tried to explain that I was "car sitting" for a friend who was serving in the Army overseas. It didn't matter. He wrote me a ticket for $200. When I went to traffic court, I waited for nearly an hour as others with tickets pled their cases. One by one, they faced the judge. They were all fined or sent to jail. I was anxious about facing the judge and trying to explain the circumstances. Clearly, I was guilty.

As I approached the bench, he asked if I was Mr. Nichols, I said yes. He shuffled some papers around, looked down at me and without any questions, declared, "Case dismissed!"

"What?" I asked. "I don't understand. You haven't even heard my explanation."

He moved his glasses to the end of his nose, looked down over the bench and said for all to hear, "Mr. Nichols, it just doesn't get any better than 'case dismissed!' Next case, please!"

This true story illustrates what is at the core of biblical forgiveness. When I drove away from the courthouse, I realized the only way I could be forgiven in God's courtroom was that Jesus Christ completely paid for my sins. Only then could God declare, "Case dismissed" for me. Jesus paid the debt I couldn't pay and gave me freedom from condemnation (Romans 8:1).

Are you convinced that your debt before God has been completely paid by Someone who had the means and the love to pay it for you? To the extent you experience the cleansing forgiveness of God, you'll be able and willing to forgive those who have hurt you.

Pastor and author Lewis Smedes that our natural desire is for revenge, but the thirst for vengeance leads only to bondage: "Vengeance is having a videotape planted in your soul that cannot be turned off. It plays the painful scene over and over again inside your mind... And each time it plays you feel the clap of pain again... Forgiving turns off the videotape of pained memory. Forgiving sets you free."[13]

The status of a loved, forgiven, cherished child of God became yours the moment you said "Yes" to Jesus Christ. That day began a lifetime of discovery. We can never plumb the depths of God's amazing grace and his purpose for us, but it's our great delight to pursue him and his will every day. That's how beloved children respond to the parents who delight in them!

Every choice to turn from selfishness to God's love and power is another brush stroke on your portrait. It's taking shape. It's already beautiful, and it's becoming lovelier every day.

Mona Hsu has served on the faculty and staff at San Diego Christian College for over thirty years. She is a faithful and capable servant with many God-given talents. She wrote this poem to illustrate how our new, God-given image takes shape.

Portrait in Progress

Each line of peace and pain,
Through our Master's skillful hand.
Stroke by stroke, line by line
He molds us slowly according to His design.
At times...
He seemingly stopped and left me aside.
Impatiently I waited and sighed.
"He must have forgotten His portrait," I cried.
At times...
He quickly added one line after another.
What was in His mind? I wondered.
Shall I be lovely, shall I be wonderful?
Softly He whispered,
"In my time,
I will finish your portrait with the image
Of my beloved Son, Jesus Christ."

Consider this . . .

1. Have you ever watched an artist paint a portrait or a landscape? Why do you think they take such pains putting in the background before they work on the main subject?

2. Describe the spiritual process of "changing clothes"? How does this metaphor help us understand the choices in repentance?

3. Which of the several examples Paul used to illustrate the metaphor can you apply today? Explain how you'll do it.

4. Which of the growth principles comes easy for you? Which one is difficult but necessary? What can you do to begin implementing it right away? What difference will it make in your life?

5. Which (if any) of the forgiveness myths have plagued you? Explain your answer.

6. As you read that section of the chapter, who came to mind that you need to forgive? From whom do you need to ask for forgiveness?

7. What are some reasons we need both persistence and patience as we apply the principles in this chapter?

A prayer . . .

Lord, thank you for your patience as I absorb your truths and learn to live by them! Open my eyes to see the "dirty clothes" I need to replace with the love and power of the gospel of grace. Help me dig deep into your grace for me so that I forgive those who have hurt me. Today, I want to change these clothes:

CHAPTER 5

The Finished Portrait

> Real Christians are marked by sincerity—the whole truth about themselves and the whole truth about God. Real Christians stand before people the way they stand before God—transparent and vulnerable. Anything less is a dressed-up Gospel.
>
> —John Fischer

Someday . . . someday the portrait will be completely finished. Not today, not tomorrow, but someday—we can be certain it will happen. It's helpful to step back and look at the entire sweep of God's purpose for the universe. The Bible depicts four movements: creation, the fall into sin, redemption, and restoration. These don't have equal weight in the pages of the Bible. The creation account is in the first two chapters of Genesis, and the fall is in chapter 3. From there until the last chapters of Revelation, God describes the beauty and power of God's work to reach sinners, draw them to himself, forgive them, and begin the process of restoration. The complete restoration—of individuals with new, glorified bodies . . . and the whole universe in the new heaven and new earth—happens at the end of the story. On that day, we'll walk in the very presence of God, thoroughly cleansed from sin, and with more joy than we can imagine. We won't spend eternity as disembodied spirits. We'll have glorified physical bodies (like Christ's after the resurrection) on a restored planet in a restored universe. The ultimate goal of God's grace, then, is the restoration of all things. Paul explained, "For God was pleased to have all his fullness dwell in [Christ], and through him to reconcile to himself all things, whether things on earth or things in heaven, by making peace through his blood, shed on the cross" (Colossians 1:19-20).

In his famous sermon, "The Weight of Glory," C. S. Lewis gives us a glimpse of what we'll enjoy. He says five things will happen: we'll be with Christ; we'll be transformed to be like Christ; we'll enjoy a lavish banquet at the family gathering of believers from every tribe, tongue, and nation; we'll experience God's glory; and we'll have meaningful work in the consummated kingdom of God. To experience "glory" doesn't mean we'll become some kind of incandescent bulb. It is, Lewis insists, what our hearts have longed for all along. We've tried to fulfill that desire with secondary things like good food, sex, money, comfort, and prestige, but all of these are just a shadow of the real thing. He told the audience that our desires today (even our misguided ones) show that we're made for something far, far more grand and glorious:

"The sense that in this universe we are treated as strangers, the longing acknowledged, to meet with some response, to bridge some chasm that yawns between us and reality, is part of our inconsolable secret. And surely, from this point of view, the promise of glory, in the sense described, becomes highly relevant to our deep desire. For glory meant good report with God, acceptance by God, acknowledgement and welcome into the heart of things. The door on which we have been knocking all our lives will open at last."[14]

Live in Light of Eternity

Throughout the Scriptures, God invites us to think, consider, reflect, and ponder the truth so that it sinks deep into our hearts and changes our attitudes and choices. Thinking of eternity isn't an easy escape from the troubles of this life. Instead, God's eternal promise gives us the courage to face painful realities with genuine hope. He assures us that our disappointments and heartaches today aren't the end of the story. No matter how bad things get, God will have the last word. In a letter to the Corinthians, Paul explained how an eternal perspective gives us courage to face today's difficulties:

> "Therefore do not lose heart, even though our outward man is perishing, yet the inward man is being renewed day by day. For our light affliction, which is but for a moment, is working for us a far more exceeding and eternal weight of glory, while we do not look at the things which are seen, but at the things which are not seen. For the things which are seen are temporary, but the things which are not seen are eternal" (2 Corinthians 4:16-18).

He may not rescue us *out of* our suffering, but he promises to be with us every step *through* it. Our struggles may not make sense to us now, but we can trust in God's infinite wisdom and kindness. Every event and every encounter today is a brush stroke in the Master's painting of our lives.

Reflecting on the ultimate outcome gives us perspective to handle today's difficulties.

> He may not rescue us out of our suffering, but he promises to be with us every step *through* it.

If you knew you were going to receive millions tomorrow, wouldn't you worry less today? If you knew you were going to win an Academy Award tomorrow, wouldn't you handle criticism better today? If you knew you were going to move next to your best friend tomorrow, couldn't you handle life's hassles better today? God's assurance is far greater than billions of dollars, awards, and time with a good friend. He promises supreme joy and fulfillment in the unfettered presence of God himself, a family feast that will bring the highest happiness, and work more meaningful than we've ever imagined . . . for all eternity.

This assurance doesn't take away today's pain, but it gives us a bedrock of confidence that God will use our pain to produce something wonderful and meaningful—if we'll trust him. Our new identity in Christ makes a difference in how we handle every situation.

- Do you feel ignored, rejected, or condemned by the people around you? Remember that the King of the universe has warmly accepted you. Treasure his love.

- Do you assume a particular failure, or a pattern of failure, has disqualified you from God's love? Think deeply about the price Christ paid to forgive sins—including yours. Thank him for his mercy and kindness.

- Do you feel alone? Consider that the omnipresent God, the one who has demonstrated the extent of his love for you by paying the ultimate price, will never leave you or forsake you. Even when you don't feel his presence, he's there.

- Do you feel hopeless, that your life doesn't matter? Remember that God is the Master Artist. He uses the dark colors of failure and heartache as the background for the brilliance of grace, hope, and a meaningful future.

- Do you feel anxious and out of control? Thank God that he holds all things in his hands, and trust him to work all things together for good. Relax. Your Father knows how to make something good out of a calamity.

We've said that our new identity "changes everything." Do you see it now? With a bedrock of security in the unchanging love of God, failure doesn't threaten us and criticism doesn't destroy us. We can love people with no manipulative strings attached. We no longer have to control them; we can let them make their own decisions. These aren't minor, incremental changes—they're category busters! When we have a new identity as loved, forgiven, accepted children of God, we have a new grid to evaluate failure and success, new eyes to see the people around us, and a new foundation to build a future that brings glory to the One who loves us!

Three Key Components

Experts agree that there are basically three essential components in a healthy self-image: a sense of belonging, a sense of worth, and a sense of competence.

A sense of belonging means that you feel accepted or acceptable. You feel warm, comforted, loved, and wanted—just as you are, unconditionally. In other words, you'll be missed when you're absent.

A sense of worth means that your life counts. You have something to offer. Your perceptions, thoughts, and opinions are important or are significant. You are worthy of respect.

A sense of competence means that you can complete a task, cope with a difficult person, and are able to handle life's difficulties. You have wisdom to make good decisions. You are affirmed as a person of good judgment.

We all have natural skills and the ability to accomplish certain things well, but we often reach our limit and face frustration. A new identity in Christ provides a wealth of God's resources of wisdom, power, love, and direction. As we learn to live according to our new identity, we tap into those resources. The direction of our lives is shaped by God's invitation and call to follow him as reflectors of his glorious image.

We use the term "calling" to mean several different things, from someone contacting us by phone to our conviction about our life's work. In his insightful book, *The Call*, Os Guinness defines our spiritual calling as "the truth that God calls us to himself so decisively that everything we are, everything we do, and everything we have is invested with a special devotion and dynamism lived out as a response to his summons and service." Our call is not primarily to a career or a type of service, or to a company or to a particular church. It is first to God himself. The impact of that relationship determines every aspect of our identity, every action we do, and how we use every resource we have.

> **The direction of our lives is shaped by God's invitation and call to follow him as reflectors of his glorious image.**

The depth and breadth of our response is shaped by the extent of our awe for the One who is calling us. Guinness reminds us, "God calls people to himself, but this call is no casual suggestion. He is so awe inspiring and his summons so commanding that only one response is appropriate—a response as total and universal as the authority of the Caller."[15]

As the Master Artist works on our portrait, it will increasingly reflect the image of Christ. The world will know we are Christians by our love. Paul wrote, "Therefore, as God's chosen people, holy and dearly loved, clothe yourselves with compassion, kindness, humility, gentleness and patience, bearing with one another. . . . And over all these virtues put on love, which binds them all together in perfect unity" (Colossians 3:12-14).

Poland's Ignace Paderewski was a remarkable musician. At one point, a mother wishing to encourage her young son's progress at the piano bought tickets for a Paderewski performance. When the night arrived, they found their seats near the front of the concert hall and eyed the majestic Steinway on stage.

Soon the mother found a friend and began a conversation. As they talked, the boy slipped away. When the time for the concert arrived, the spotlights came on, and the audience quieted. At that moment, the mother noticed her son sitting on stage at the piano! He began playing "Twinkle, Twinkle, Little Star."

His mother gasped, but before she could retrieve her son, Paderewski appeared on the stage and sat next to the boy. "Don't quit—keep playing," he whispered. Paderewski reached down with his left hand and began filling in a bass part. Soon his right arm reached around the other side, encircling the child, to add a running obbligato. Together, the old master and the young novice held the crowd mesmerized."[16]

In our lives—as incompetent and incomplete as we sometimes feel—the Master surrounds us with confidence, courage, and compassion. And when the challenges of life become overwhelming, he whispers in our ear: "Don't quit—don't quit. I will see that the portrait is completed with amazing beauty."

Ambidextrous Faith

The lies of the enemy, the temptations of our human nature, and the incessant shouts of advertising all try to get to erode our trust in a good and sovereign God. We may not understand what God is doing, but trust doesn't demand complete answers. We only need one answer: that God loves us and will use everything for our good and his glory. Every moment is a gift or a lesson. If we misinterpret the lesson God is teaching us, we may spiral down into doubt, discouragement, disappointment, and possibly even depression. If we believe that we are exempt from struggles or that it's God's job to protect us from them, we will slide down that chute pretty quickly. In *Reaching for the Invisible God*, Philip Yancey states, "Gregory of Nyssa once called St. Basil's faith 'ambidextrous' because he welcomed pleasures with the right hand and afflictions with the left, convinced that both would serve God's design for him."[17]

Where does this kind of faith come from? It doesn't just happen by osmosis. Faith is a muscle that must be exercised to grow strong. Faith grows as we spend time contemplating the wonders of God—not in passing or occasionally, but to reshape our thinking and begin to be amazed. Only then does our new identity and an eternal perspective transform our hearts and our lives. Pastor and author John Ortberg commented about the necessity of worship and its impact on his life.

> "I need to worship because without it I can forget that I have a Big God beside me and live in fear. I need to worship because without it I can forget his calling and begin to live in a spirit of self-preoccupation. I need to worship because without it I lose a sense of wonder and gratitude and plod through life with blinders on. I need worship because my natural tendency is toward self-reliance and stubborn independence."[18]

All of us need the reminder that God delights in restoring broken people. But first, we have to be honest enough to admit we're broken. The Duke of Norfolk once sent the priceless Portland Vase to the king of England as an expression of his esteem. The king placed the vase in the British Museum for all to enjoy. Back at the Duke's home, a servant was dismissed when it was revealed that he was plotting to overthrow the Duke. Livid with hatred, the servant vowed to get his revenge. He traveled to the British Museum in London. He watched carefully as visitors filed by the priceless vase. When there were no visitors in the area and the attendants were out of sight, the servant grasped the beautiful masterpiece, raised it above his head and smashed it to the floor.

Attendants rushed to the scene, but it was too late. The Portland Vase was smashed into a thousand pieces.

When the king heard the news he was both shocked and grieved, but he commanded, "Save every piece. This is my most precious and treasured gift. We'll search for a man who can repair it, no matter what it costs."

It took a long time to find a craftsman whose skills were worthy of the task. He turned out to be a distant relative of the original creator of the vase. He came to London and, piece by tiny piece, he restored the vase so that only tiny scars can be seen that attest to its repair.[19] It was placed back in the museum where it can be seen today.

The Master Artist, your Creator God, also sent a relative, his only begotten Son, to restore your brokenness to the original glory of his creation. Healing will leave some scars, but these will attest to God's loving restoration. Our scars are precious because of the scars the Son of God bore when the Evil One tried to destroy him on the cross where he gave his life so that you could be fully restored.

Because of Christ, you are deeply loved, completely forgiven, and totally accepted as God's beloved son or daughter. Soak in it, bask in it, and live according to it. You are a trophy of God's amazing grace.

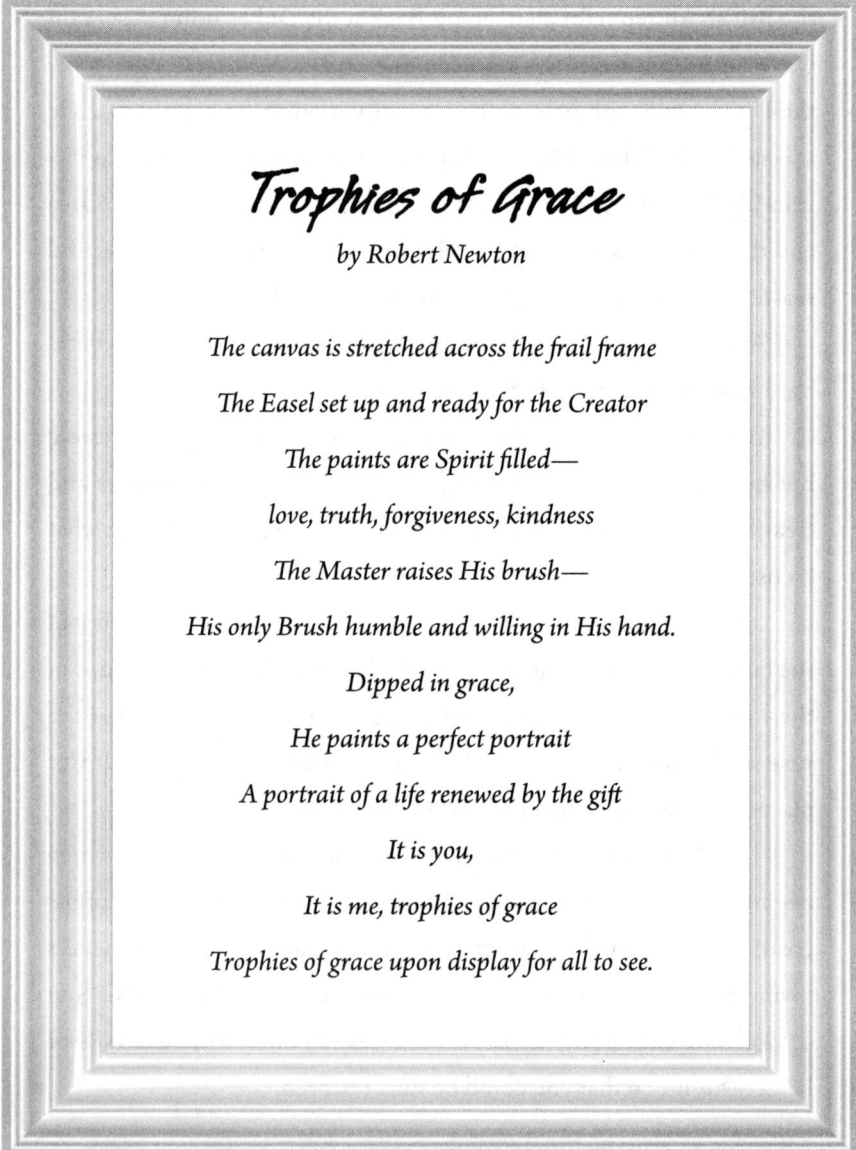

Trophies of Grace
by Robert Newton

The canvas is stretched across the frail frame
The Easel set up and ready for the Creator
The paints are Spirit filled—
love, truth, forgiveness, kindness
The Master raises His brush—
His only Brush humble and willing in His hand.
Dipped in grace,
He paints a perfect portrait
A portrait of a life renewed by the gift
It is you,
It is me, trophies of grace
Trophies of grace upon display for all to see.

Consider this . . .

1. How does it (or could it) encourage you to know that someday your portrait will be completely finished?

2. Lewis identifies five things that will happen to you then (we'll be with Christ, like Christ, feast, glory, and meaningful work). Why does the assurance of these things matter now?

3. How does your new identity in Christ give you a greater sense of belonging, worth, and competence?

4. How would you describe "ambidextrous faith"? On a scale of 0 (nonexistent) to 10 (all day every day), how much of your life is characterized by an ambidextrous trust in God? Explain your answer.

5. How does real, rigorous, deep worship refocus our hearts and change our lives? What are some specific ways you can experience this kind of worship more fully and more often?

6. What are two or three of the most important principles you've learned from this book? How have they begun to change your life? How do you expect them to change it even more?

A prayer . . .
Lord Jesus, someday I'll see you face-to-face! What a wonderful day that will be! Before then, I want to experience a deeper sense of belonging to you, being loved by you, and sharpening the talents you've given me—so that my life increasingly reflects your character. Today, Lord, I'm thankful for . . .

Endnotes

1 Larry Crabb, *The Safest Place on Earth: Where People Connect and Are Forever Changed* (Thomas Nelson: Nashville, 1999).

2 Robert McGee, *Search for Significance* (Thomas Nelson: Nashville, 1998).

3 Cited at jan.ucc.nau.edu/~jsa3/hum355/readings/ellul.htm.

4 "The Power of Advertising," Monita Rajpal, CNN, cited on www.cnn.com/2010/WORLD/europe/09/22/power.of.advertising/index.html.

5 "All about Madonna," *Vanity Fair*, April 1991.

6 Cited by James Dobson in *Bringing Up Girls* (Tyndale, 2010), p. 16.

7 *60 Minutes*, November 6, 2005.

8 C. S. Lewis, *The Screwtape Letters* (HarperOne: New York, 2009), Preface.

9 Henry Scougal, *The Life of God in the Soul of Man*, cited at www.lamblion.net/Quotations/scougal_henry.html.

10 Adapted, source unknown.

11 Gerald G. May, *The Awakened Heart* (HarperCollins: New York, 1991).

12 You can order my booklet on forgiveness from aliveministries.net

13 Lewis Smedes, *Quiet Times for Couples* (Harvest House Publishers: Eugene, Oregon, 1990), 91.

14 C. S. Lewis, "The Weight of Glory," a sermon preached on June 8, 1942, online at www.verber.com/mark/xian/weight-of-glory.pdf

15 Os Guinness, *The Call*, (Word Publishing: Nashville, 1998), pp. 4, 30.

16 "Illustrations for Preaching and Teaching," *Leadership Journal* (Grand Rapids, MI: Baker Books, 1993), p. 221.

17 Phillip Yancey, *Reaching for the Invisible God* (Grand Rapids: Zondervan, 2000), p. 69.

18 John Ortberg, *If You Want to Walk on Water, You Have to Get Out of the Boat* (Grand Rapids: Zondervan, 2001).

19 Wolf Mankowitz, *The Portland Vase and the Wedgwood Copies* (1954).

Alive Resources

For more copies of this book and for many other helpful resources, visit www.aliveministries.net

Now, about those 50 push-ups . . . Did you believe me? The answer to the question on page 55 in the book is: Yes, indeed! I can still do 50 push-ups even at this senior season of life! I do five a day over a ten-day period! It's the same accomplishment, just a different, age-sensitive strategy.